STRENGTHEN
YOUR HANDS

*How Godly Leaders Remain Strong
in the Work of the Lord*

PAUL CHAPPELL

First published in 2015 by Striving Together Publications, a ministry
of Lancaster Baptist Church, Lancaster, CA 93535. Striving Together
Publications is committed to providing tried, trusted, and proven
resources that will further equip local churches to carry out the
Great Commission. Your comments and suggestions are valued.

Striving Together Publications
4020 E. Lancaster Blvd.
Lancaster, CA 93535
800.201.7748
strivingtogether.com

Cover design by Andrew Jones
Layout by Craig Parker
Writing assistance by Monica Bass

The author and publication team have put forth every effort to give
proper credit to quotes and thoughts that are not original with the
author. It is not our intent to claim originality with any quote or
thought that could not readily be tied to an original source.

ISBN 978-1-59894-295-8
Printed in the United States of America

Table of Contents

Introduction v

1. Remember the Source of Strength 1

2. Commit to a Purpose Larger than Yourself . . 13

3. Set Direction through Organization 23

4. Practice Teamwork 33

5. Look beyond the Rubbish 41

6. Persist through Opposition 51

7. Refuse To Compromise 61

8. Anchor Your Hope in God's Word 73

9. Find Your Joy in the Lord 81

10. Give Thanks 89

Conclusion 97

Introduction
Strengthen My Hands

Beginning—it usually comes with a surge of adrenaline blunting the realities that we are in over our heads.

And then the truth sets in. And fatigue. Faith falters, and hope wanes.

What was I thinking? I can't handle this responsibility.

Truthfully, as spiritual leaders, we have monumental tasks before us. Whether you are a parent, teacher, pastor, Sunday school class teacher, ministry helper, or any Christian leading others in any area, you have been entrusted with responsibilities beyond human ability—

reaching the world with the gospel, shepherding young hearts for God, changing lives, building a church, nurturing spiritual growth. And with each of these responsibilities comes obstacles unique to your situation.

It's easy to become overwhelmed and to find ourselves weak in the most vital callings. After all, what is one person against so great a task?

You know the standard answer: With God's calling comes God's enabling.

It's more than a cliché—it's truth, paraphrased from 1 Thessalonians 5:24: "Faithful is he that calleth you, who also will do it." But how do we experience this truth on the most practical levels? What do we do when our hands are weak but the needs are great?

We find answers to these questions in the life of one of the great leaders of the Bible—Nehemiah. I love the book of Nehemiah for many reasons: It tells us the impossible can be accomplished with God. It speaks to building for God's glory and refusing to compromise with the world. It is perhaps the most condensed practical volume on leadership principles in the world. And one of the lessons that we learn from Nehemiah is how to stay strong in the work of the Lord.

Nehemiah faced an overwhelming task and was bombarded with relentless opposition. Yet we see in his leadership a level of determination, persistence, and reliance upon God that led to the completion of one of the greatest building programs in history.

How did he do it? How did he keep from giving up in despair or caving in to pressure?

I believe we find a large part of the answer in Nehemiah 6:9: "For they all made us afraid, saying, Their hands shall be weakened from the work, that it be not done. Now therefore, O God, strengthen my hands."

Strengthen my hands.

Throughout the book of Nehemiah we glean practical lessons on how this leader kept himself focused and encouraged—how he drew strength from the Lord.

In these pages, we'll draw applications on how, in basic, practical ways, we can strengthen our hands in the work of the Lord. Some lessons we'll draw from a specific passage, and some we'll note reoccurring throughout Nehemiah's life. This is not an expository resource on the book of Nehemiah. It's not even exhaustive on the topic of strengthening our hands. It is written simply to give you ten practical—and biblically proven—ways to remain strong in the work which God has called you to do.

Chapter One
Remember the Source of Strength

"My life is one long daily, hourly record of answered prayer. For physical health, for mental overstrain, for guidance given marvelously, for errors and dangers averted, for enmity to the gospel subdued, for food provided at the exact hour needed, for everything that goes to make up life and my poor service, I can testify with a full and often wonder-stricken awe that God answers prayer." Such was the testimony of Mary Slessor, missionary in West Africa from 1876–1915.

The needs Mary Slessor mentioned are the very needs you and I face. And the resource she mentioned is the very resource of which we make too little use.

Indeed, prayer is the key resource which God has given us to strengthen our hands for the work. When we labor in our strength, we deplete ourselves. When we labor in God's power, we receive His sustaining energy and His blessing on our tasks.

Even the strongest leaders find themselves overwhelmed by the needs they are called to meet. It's part and parcel of leadership. The very reason you are a leader is because there is a need, but God does not ask you to meet those needs in your strength.

And yet, many of us have a distinct tendency to labor in *our* strength. We see the needs around us, and we jump in to help. We begin projects, carry burdens, serve people, face challenges—all in the weakness of human strength.

But there is one source of lasting strength, and it is availed through prayer. Prayer is the amazing line God has provided for direct access to His throne where He provides both sympathy and power.

> For we have not an high priest which cannot
> be touched with the feeling of our infirmities;
> but was in all points tempted like as we are,

yet without sin. Let us therefore come boldly unto the throne of grace, that we may obtain mercy, and find grace to help in time of need.
—HEBREWS 4:15–16

D. L. Moody once said, "Next to the wonder of seeing my Savior will be, I think, the wonder that I made so little use of the power of prayer." Truly, it is a resource of which we should avail ourselves continually.

The book of Nehemiah is a study on prayer. Throughout these thirteen chapters, there are eight specific occurrences recorded of Nehemiah's seeking God's help through prayer:

- He prayed when confronted with need (Nehemiah 1:4–11).
- He prayed for wisdom (Nehemiah 2:4).
- He prayed in adversity (Nehemiah 4:4–5).
- He prayed for God's reward (Nehemiah 5:19).
- He prayed for strength (Nehemiah 6:9).
- He prayed for deliverance from enemies (Nehemiah 6:14).
- He prayed with God's people (Nehemiah 9:5–38).
- He prayed for God's remembrance (Nehemiah 13:14, 22, 29, 30).

In every need, Nehemiah's first response was prayer. In fact, that is the first truth we learn from Nehemiah on strengthening our hands through prayer: it starts with a need.

Prayer begins with need

We are introduced to Nehemiah at a moment when he hears devastating news. He is serving in the palace court where the Jews are in captivity. Nehemiah's brother, Hanani, returned from the city of Jerusalem, some two thousand miles away, and described the ruin and reproach of the city.

> The words of Nehemiah the son of Hachaliah. And it came to pass in the month Chisleu, in the twentieth year, as I was in Shushan the palace, That Hanani, one of my brethren, came, he and certain men of Judah; and I asked them concerning the Jews that had escaped, which were left of the captivity, and concerning Jerusalem. And they said unto me, The remnant that are left of the captivity there in the province are in great affliction and reproach: the wall of Jerusalem also is broken down, and the gates thereof are burned with fire.—NEHEMIAH 1:1–3

Have you ever considered that every miracle began with a problem? That every answer to prayer begins with a need?

The inverse, however, is not always true. Not every problem results in God's intervention, and not every need is answered with God's touch. The reason for this is simple: we often don't pray.

Nehemiah, upon hearing the need in Jerusalem, did what every godly leader will do—he prayed.

> And it came to pass, when I heard these words, that I sat down and wept, and mourned certain days, and fasted, and prayed before the God of heaven,—NEHEMIAH 1:4

Nehemiah repeatedly faced overwhelming obstacles as a leader—from within and without. And every time, the needs drove Nehemiah—not to human help—but to his knees in prayer. Prayer was his first response, not his last resort.

Prayer is a priority

We are so busy. The great evangelist R. A. Torrey said, "We are too busy to pray, and so we are too busy to have power. We have a great deal of activity but accomplish little. We have many services but few conversions. We have much machinery but few results."

Leaders today are constantly on call, and, thanks to technology, we are constantly available. Our schedules are full, but our souls are empty. The needs in front of us are great, but our ability to continue in prayer is feeble. No wonder our hands are weak. We are simply too busy, too overwhelmed, too driven to seek the face of God.

You've heard of George Müller—the man of great faith who saw God provide for thousands of orphans he took into his care. Müller was a busy man, but he made prayer a priority. In his words, "For more than half a century, I have never known one day when I had not more business than I could get through. For forty years, I have had annually about 30,000 letters, and most of these have passed through my own hands. I have nine assistants always at work corresponding in German, French, English, Danish, Italian, Russian, and other languages. Then, as pastor of a church with 1,200 believers, great has been my care. I have had charge of five orphanages; also at my publishing depot, the printing and circulation of millions of tracts, books, and Bibles. But I have always made it a rule never to begin work till I have had a good season with God."

John Bunyan, author of *Pilgrim's Progress,* wrote, "He who runs from God in the morning will scarcely find Him the rest of the day." Our days should begin with a humble seeking of God's help and power. God knows the struggles we face each day. He understands the temptations and pitfalls awaiting us. And He alone can help us overcome life's problems.

Could it be that our hands are weak because we have neglected private prayer? It is the source of both personal strength and of divine intervention.

Prayer is effective through fervency

For Nehemiah, prayer was no mere ritual. It was the pouring out of a heart-felt burden. He wept and mourned. He fasted. His was the prayer of an exercised soul, moved with a heart for God's glory and with compassion for God's people.

Jesus, too, saw needs and was moved with compassion for them. Mark 6:34 says, "And Jesus, when he came out, saw much people, and was moved with compassion toward them, because they were as sheep not having a shepherd: and he began to teach them many things."

Sometimes when we are overwhelmed as leaders our tendency is to shut out the needs around us—to become oblivious, calloused, or even cynical. What if we instead let the burdens piled on our shoulders drive us to fervency in prayer? James 5:16 promises, "The effectual fervent prayer of a righteous man availeth much."

Prayer claims God's promises

In 1986, God called my wife and me to serve a small, struggling congregation in Lancaster, California. The church had fewer than twenty members, and, unbeknownst to us, the building they owned was in foreclosure. As we prayed and labored and witnessed, the Lord began to grow our church. Miraculously, just five years later, our church embarked on a great journey of faith as we purchased land and began construction on a larger building.

The story of that building program would be a book in itself—a book describing problems, insufficiencies, and burdens beyond our ability to manage. To give you an idea, the story includes our general contractor's going bankrupt and the foreman's of the construction crew fleeing the state with the only set of blueprints we had and the bank's canceling our loan. It also includes a pastor still under thirty years old driven to desperation over and over again.

One afternoon, a salesman from a pew company left a small sample pew for me to show our congregation as a money-raising visual. That Sunday night I explained to our church family that I would place the pew and a clipboard in the middle of the new building. I asked our people to go when they could throughout the week and kneel at the "prayer pew" to pray for God's provision and help. I also suggested that they write their names and the times they prayed on the clipboard.

I still have the papers our people signed on that clipboard. They record times as early as 1:00 AM and 2:00 AM, and they are stained with tears.

This season of prayer was the turning point for our building program. Through a miraculous series of events, God provided the funds to continue the work, and the rest of the story, although not without difficulties, is a testimony to the incredible faithfulness of God.

It also turned out to be a preface in an ongoing story of God's provision for our church family. Since that first building program, we have had need to build one new building after another as the Lord has blessed our outreach and expanded our membership.

I can't tell you how many times over the years in the midst of a building program I've cried out to God, "Lord, this is not our church, it is Yours. And You promised, 'I will build *my* church' (Matthew 16:18). And so, Lord, we claim this promise and ask you to build—not simply buildings, but lives. We ask You to provide the resources we need to move forward for You in the ongoing labor of building Your church."

Space does not permit me to recount all the ways which God has answered those prayers. I can tell you, however, that in the current building we are constructing—a $9 million project—we have a prayer bench. And I can tell you that the tear-stained pages in the three-ring binder by the bench are testimony to a church of people who still claim God's promises in prayer.

This is how Nehemiah prayed. He reminded God of His promises and claimed them as he prayed.

> Remember, I beseech thee, the word that thou commandedst thy servant Moses, saying, If ye transgress, I will scatter you abroad among the nations: But if ye turn unto me, and keep my commandments, and do them; though there were of you cast out unto the uttermost part of the heaven, yet will I gather them from thence, and will bring them unto the place that I have chosen to set my name there.—NEHEMIAH 1:8–9

What promise do you need to claim as you pray?

Are you in need of courage? Claim Joshua 1:9 as you pray: "Have not I commanded thee? Be strong and of a good courage; be not afraid, neither be thou dismayed: for the LORD thy God is with thee whithersoever thou goest."

Are you in need of hope? Claim Romans 15:13 as you pray: "Now the God of hope fill you with all joy and peace in believing, that ye may abound in hope, through the power of the Holy Ghost."

Are you in need of strength? Claim 2 Corinthians 12:9 as you pray: "And he said unto me, My grace is sufficient for thee: for my strength is made perfect in weakness. Most gladly therefore will I rather glory in my infirmities, that the power of Christ may rest upon me."

Are you in need of peace? Claim Isaiah 26:3 as you pray: "Thou wilt keep him in perfect peace, whose mind is stayed on thee: because he trusteth in thee."

Are you in need of wisdom? Claim James 1:5 as you pray: "If any of you lack wisdom, let him ask of God, that giveth to all men liberally, and upbraideth not; and it shall be given him."

Ransack God's Word for His promises, and use them in your prayers. "For all the promises of God in him are yea, and in him Amen, unto the glory of God by us" (2 Corinthians 1:20).

Prayer is powerful

The book of Nehemiah is not only a study on prayer; it is a record of *answered* prayers. Through prayer, Nehemiah saw the walls of Jerusalem erected in just *fifty-two days*. This was the work of over a million laborers with a courageous leader who dared believe that God would answer prayer and who dared to pray in the face of every need.

What about you? Are the needs great? Cry out to God. Spend time daily seeking His face and strength.

> Hearken unto the voice of my cry, my King, and my God: for unto thee will I pray. My voice shalt thou hear in the morning, O LORD; in the morning will I direct my prayer unto thee, and will look up.—PSALM 5:2–3

When your hands are weak, remember the source of strength; and avail yourself of that strength through prayer.

Then I told them of the hand of my God which was good upon me; as also the king's words that he had spoken unto me. And they said, Let us rise up and build. So they strengthened their hands for this good work.—Nehemiah 2:18

"All God's giants have been weak men who did great things for God because they reckoned on God being with them."
—Hudson Taylor

Chapter Two
Commit to a Purpose Larger than Yourself

Winston Churchill once said, "There comes a moment in everyone's life: a moment for which that person was born. That special opportunity, when he seizes it, will fulfill his mission, a mission for which he was uniquely qualified."

Certainly, Nehemiah was a man who lived out his purpose. As God opened doors of opportunity, Nehemiah walked through them with full commitment to his God, the people he was called to serve, and the task before him.

This level of commitment to a clear purpose has a way of strengthening us in the work of the Lord. What does it take to develop a clear sense of purpose and to commit fully to it?

See with eyes of compassion

In a day when people are mugged while citizens pass by and when churches are closing and no one seems to care, I believe God is looking for people with the ability to feel deeply.

As we saw in our last chapter, Nehemiah was such a man. He had the compassion to pray and to care.

All of us have some measure of compassion. Perhaps it is simply experiencing a moment of sadness for the pain of someone else. But biblical compassion is more than that. It is feeling the needs of others as if they were your own. As someone once said, "Compassion is your hurt in my heart." This is the level of compassion which Nehemiah exercised.

It was Nehemiah's compassion that set off the course of events which led to his moment of purpose and mission. For it was compassion that led Nehemiah to make a trip from the palace to Jerusalem to "seek the welfare of the children of Israel" (Nehemiah 2:10). He deeply cared about people.

If we look for our purpose through eyes of personal fulfillment, we'll miss it every time. We'll sell ourselves short on selfish aspirations. But if we look for our purpose through eyes of compassion, we'll find it in the needs surrounding us.

Find direction from God

Of course, need alone does not dictate our purpose. When we go that route, we find ourselves frazzled, depleted, and with little to show for our efforts.

Nehemiah knew better, and so he spent time alone with God during his survey trip. Nehemiah 2:12 records, "And I arose in the night, I and some few men with me; neither told I any man what my God had put in my heart to do at Jerusalem: neither was there any beast with me, save the beast that I rode upon."

This communion with God alone is where ministry begins. As Leonard Ravenhill said, "To be much for God we must be much with God." Godly leaders spend time seeking the face of God and waiting for Him for purpose and direction. They let God place both the burden and the solution on their hearts. And they are willing to spend time alone with and waiting for the Lord until this happens.

In coming days, Nehemiah would face tremendous opposition. He couldn't possibly have known just how fierce the opposition would be, but he did know that objections would come. He knew that he needed a clear purpose and promise from God before he could face the obstacles.

When we seek God for direction, sometimes He leads in ways we do not anticipate. But always He leads with clarity and toward the needs of others.

Because Nehemiah spent time alone with God, he had a crystal clear purpose. His stated mission was two-fold:

- **To restore the structure of the walls:** "And I went out by night by the gate of the valley, even before the dragon well, and to the dung port, and viewed the walls of Jerusalem, which were broken down, and the gates thereof were consumed with fire. Then I went on to the gate of the fountain, and to the king's pool: but there was no place for the beast that was under me to pass" (Nehemiah 2:13–14).

- **To restore the strength of the nation:** "Then said I unto them, Ye see the distress that we are in, how Jerusalem lieth waste, and the gates thereof are burned with fire: come, and let us build up the wall of Jerusalem, that we be no more a reproach" (Nehemiah 2:17).

The charred, broken-down walls were not only unsafe, but they were a shame to God's testimony and to God's people. Like David who entered combat with Goliath to defend the name of God, Nehemiah's heart burned for God's glory to be restored in the eyes of others.

Exercise courage

The clarity of Nehemiah's mission called for courage, and he didn't shirk. It wasn't the fact that Nehemiah was a leader that called forth his courage. It was Nehemiah's courage that called forth his leadership. Nehemiah had a comfy "government job," but he saw a need, and took the lead.

Courage is not the absence of fear; it is overcoming our fears to meet the needs around us and do the will of God.

If you are serving as a leader, I can guarantee that you experience times of well-founded fears. But as you spend time alone with God, as He confirms His purpose in your life, and as you remember who God is, you can exercise courage.

Hear God's Word to Joshua, and draw strength from it: "Have not I commanded thee? Be strong and of a good courage; be not afraid, neither be thou dismayed: for the

LORD thy God is with thee whithersoever thou goest" (Joshua 1:9).

Commit fully

Nothing of lasting value is accomplished by half-hearted measures.

Nehemiah didn't simply decide to "do what I can." He fully committed to build the walls, calling others to join him: "Then said I unto them, Ye see the distress that we are in, how Jerusalem lieth waste, and the gates thereof are burned with fire: come, and let us build up the wall of Jerusalem, that we be no more a reproach" (Nehemiah 2:17).

Nothing weakens our hands like indecision and half-hearted contributions. And nothing strengthens our hands—as well as the hands of others—like full commitment to the purpose before us.

Hope in God

One of the benefits of having a purpose greater than your resources is that it forces you to depend on God. Indeed, it was the assurance of God's presence and His hand in this endeavor that specifically prompted the people to "strengthen their hands" for the work before them. It was as Nehemiah recounted to them God's blessing that they chose to hope in God: "Then I told them of the hand of my God which was good upon me; as also the king's words that he had spoken unto me. And they said, Let us rise up and build. So they strengthened their hands for this good work" (Nehemiah 2:18).

Later, the people would become discouraged and disheartened as they looked at the rubbish surrounding them and the enemies of God threatening them. But as long as they anchored their hope in God, their hands were strong to accomplish their mission.

The hand of God is still not shortened. He doesn't only strengthen hands to build ancient walls. Today, He helps us as we labor to build through the gospel of Christ. The book of Acts records one incident after another of God's power to build the church through people who embraced His calling and depended on His power. Chapter 11 describes a group of unnamed followers of Christ who, under severe persecution, boldly proclaimed the gospel *with the help of the Lord.*

> Now they which were scattered abroad upon the persecution that arose about Stephen travelled as far as Phenice, and Cyprus, and Antioch, preaching the word to none but unto the Jews

only. And some of them were men of Cyprus and Cyrene, which, when they were come to Antioch, spake unto the Grecians, preaching the Lord Jesus. And the hand of the Lord was with them: and a great number believed, and turned unto the Lord.—ACTS 11:19–21

Did you catch that phrase, "And the hand of the Lord was with them"? The God of Nehemiah is still our hope and help today.

God's power does not end where our difficulties begin. Nehemiah faced tremendous economic need and shortness of resources. But God is not immobilized by such trifles. He provided for His purpose through the supplies of the king (Nehemiah 2:8). As Hudson Taylor testified, "God's work done in God's way will never lack God's supply."

And if God's power is not stopped by hurting economies, it is also not stopped by howling enemies. Nehemiah's declaration to build the walls may have been greeted with cheers and promises of assistance by the Jews, but "when Sanballat the Horonite, and Tobiah the servant, the Ammonite, and Geshem the Arabian, heard it, they laughed us to scorn, and despised us, and said, What is this thing that ye do? will ye rebel against the king?"

(Nehemiah 2:19). Threaten, accuse, attack, or tempt as the enemies would do, they could not prevail.

Nehemiah's hands were made strong by commitment. He knew God's purpose, and he set his hope firmly in God as he fully invested himself in accomplishing God's calling on his life.

Chapter Three
Set Direction through Organization

In the pine forests of Europe and Central and South America lives a curious insect known as the pine processionary caterpillar. This creature is so named because of its unique method of traveling across the forest—in a single-file line with other processionaries.

In the late 1890s, scientist Jean-Henri Fabre performed a legendary experiment with these caterpillars. Positioning one after the other around the rim of a flower pot so they formed a complete circle, he watched to see how long they would travel without breaking formation. In the middle of the flower pot, he placed pine needles—their food.

Amazingly, the caterpillars continued around the circle for a solid week—day and night. Their journey only ended as they died of exhaustion and starvation. With an abundance of food less than six inches away, they starved to death because they confused activity with accomplishment.[1]

The truth is, activity and accomplishment are not the same. Enthusiasm alone is not as productive as enthusiasm with a goal. One of Nehemiah's great strengths as a leader was his ability to set goals and provide an organized structure in which they could be accomplished.

God honors organization, as we see throughout Scripture. Even when Jesus wanted to bless thousands of people with a miraculous lunch, He asked His disciples to organize the event.

> …And he said to his disciples, Make them sit down by fifties in a company. And they did so, and made them all sit down. Then he took the five loaves and the two fishes, and looking up to heaven, he blessed them, and brake, and gave to the disciples to set before the multitude.
> —LUKE 9:14–16

If Nehemiah had attempted to rebuild the walls of Jerusalem without first counting the cost, preparing supplies, and organizing the efforts of others, the story would have ended differently. There was no way he could have anticipated every need and difficulty which he would face. But he was far more prepared to face the challenges outside of his control because he wasn't flustered and distracted by the ones he *could* manage.

Without clear goals, we flounder in our zeal, our compassion lacks direction, and we aren't prepared to receive God's blessings. Furthermore, we grow weary of spinning our wheels and running in circles.

Although it sometimes runs contrary to our first impulses, taking time to prepare and organize will strengthen our hands in the long run. How did Nehemiah do it?

He strategized

You remember the story: Nehemiah heard of the desolate condition of Jerusalem, fasted, and prayed; and then King Artaxerxes noticed that Nehemiah's countenance was sad and questioned him about it.

Interestingly, although it does not appear that Nehemiah was ready for that moment of conversation, he had been thinking the matter through so thoroughly that he was prepared to give the king a specific time period for his proposed survey trip.

> And I said unto the king, If it please the king, and if thy servant have found favour in thy sight, that thou wouldest send me unto Judah, unto the city of my fathers' sepulchres, that I may build it. And the king said unto me, (the queen also sitting by him,) For how long shall thy journey be? and when wilt thou return? So it pleased the king to send me; and I set him a time.—NEHEMIAH 2:5–6

This request approved, Nehemiah was ready to make petition for the next part of his plans.

> Moreover I said unto the king, If it please the king, let letters be given me to the governors beyond the river, that they may convey me over till I come into Judah; And a letter unto Asaph the keeper of the king's forest, that he may give me timber to make beams for the gates of the palace which appertained to the house, and for the wall of the city, and for the house that I shall enter into. And the king granted me,

according to the good hand of my God upon me.
—NEHEMIAH 2:7–8

Nehemiah had been doing his homework. His was a purpose with a strategy. He was so thorough in his forward thinking and his research that he not only knew how long such a journey would take but he knew who else needed to be involved and what supplies he would need. When the moment came in which he could act, he was ready.

He analyzed

With the king's blessing, Nehemiah's next step was on-site calculations. After arriving in Jerusalem, he spent significant time personally and prayerfully analyzing the needs before him.

> So I came to Jerusalem, and was there three days. And I arose in the night, I and some few men with me; neither told I any man what my God had put in my heart to do at Jerusalem: neither was there any beast with me, save the beast that I rode upon. And I went out by night by the gate of the valley, even before the dragon well, and to the dung port, and viewed the walls of Jerusalem, which were broken down, and the gates thereof

were consumed with fire. Then I went on to the gate of the fountain, and to the king's pool: but there was no place for the beast that was under me to pass. Then went I up in the night by the brook, and viewed the wall, and turned back, and entered by the gate of the valley, and so returned. And the rulers knew not whither I went, or what I did; neither had I as yet told it to the Jews, nor to the priests, nor to the nobles, nor to the rulers, nor to the rest that did the work.

—NEHEMIAH 2:11–16

Nehemiah didn't make a big scene in the analyzing stage of the project. But he carefully surveyed the need and determined how he could motivate others and organize the resources at his disposal to reach his goal.

He organized

Only after prayer, planning, and as thorough an analysis as possible did Nehemiah invite others to join him in this great work.

Then said I unto them, Ye see the distress that we are in, how Jerusalem lieth waste, and the gates thereof are burned with fire: come, and

let us build up the wall of Jerusalem, that we be no more a reproach. Then I told them of the hand of my God which was good upon me; as also the king's words that he had spoken unto me. And they said, Let us rise up and build. So they strengthened their hands for this good work.
—Nehemiah 2:17–18

Here was a leader who understood the need and had a solution.

You've seen leaders who only understood the need but had no solutions. We call them pessimists.

You've seen leaders who have solutions but don't understand the depth of the need. We call them optimists.

But Nehemiah was a faith-filled realist. He knew exactly how desperate the situation was, and he had carefully and prayerfully considered a plan that would allow the people to overcome the reality in front of them.

No wonder they wanted to help Nehemiah. No wonder they strengthened their hands for this "good work."

Nehemiah wasn't content just to do "something." Rather, he knew how to do something that mattered—that would make a difference. He didn't invest activity without a goal for accomplishment, and he didn't start without a plan for execution.

Reach for the goal

Planning and organization are necessary in all of our lives—whether we are embarking on a new endeavor or working to be faithful in the leadership role in which we already serve. "God is not the author of confusion" (1 Corinthians 14:33), and organized action is glorifying to Him.

Frankly, we weaken our hands by disorganization. We weaken our ability to respond to needs and to work efficiently when we're not able to find what we need or are not prepared for the next task at hand. We weaken our teams by failing to organize a plan of action to meet specific goals. We weaken our own resolve by investing high levels of energy with little direction.

So take stock of your activity. Do you know where you are going? Do you have a plan to get there?

Many of us could take a cue from Nehemiah in pulling away from the daily pressures to analyze prayerfully the needs we are called to meet and the people we are entrusted to serve. Life tends to disorder, thus we must constantly work to keep our plans, teams, and resources organized for maximum effect.

Taking time to set goals and organize your resources to meet them will strengthen your hands to continue in the work God has called you to accomplish.

---

1. Zig Ziglar, *See You at the Top, 25th Anniversary Edition* (Pelican Publishing Incorporated, 2005), 150.

> *They which builded on the wall, and they that bare burdens,*
> *with those that laded, every one with one of his hands wrought*
> *in the work, and with the other hand held a weapon.*
> —Nehemiah 4:17

> "There is no limit to what a man can do or where he can go if
> he doesn't mind who gets the credit."—Ronald Reagan

Chapter Four
Practice Teamwork

In an old *Peanuts* cartoon, Lucy demanded her brother Linus change the television channel.

"What makes you think you can walk right in here and take over?" asked Linus.

"These five fingers," said Lucy, holding up her hand. "Individually they are nothing, but when I curl them together like this into a single unit, they form a weapon that is terrible to behold."

"What channel do you want?" sighed Linus. Turning away, he looked at his fingers and said, "Why can't you guys get organized like that?"

Whether it's fingers on Lucy's hand, players on a sports team, or servants in the local church, teamwork makes a difference.

The turning point for Nehemiah's building project was the declaration of God's people, "Let us rise up and build" (Nehemiah 2:18). Prior to this moment, the broken-down walls had been one man's burden. Nehemiah had prayed and fasted and agonized and planned and strategized. But until he invited others to help him and until the others jumped in to help, it was nothing more than a dream. Without the work of a team, the walls could never have been erected.

That's how it works. Building God's way always involves others.

God never intended that local church work be accomplished only by the pastor, deacons, or the paid staff. In fact, the work of local church leaders is primarily that of equipping *others* to serve the Lord: "And he gave some, apostles; and some, prophets; and some, evangelists; and some, pastors and teachers; For the perfecting of the saints, for the work of the ministry, for the edifying of the body of Christ" (Ephesians 4:11–12).

Sometimes as leaders, rather than inviting others to join us in the work of the Lord, we develop a Messiah complex—a sense that our calling is to do it all. Not only does this limit God's work and those we are responsible to lead, but it weakens our own hands. We become burdened and overwhelmed and career toward burnout.

Someone once said, "It is only as we develop others around us that we permanently succeed." And thus, in God's plan, involving others in the work of the ministry is a win-win proposition: it allows them to serve in God's work, and it strengthens our hands as well.

From Nehemiah we learn key lessons on leading and serving with a team.

It takes everyone's giving all

Nehemiah 3 lists forty-one team leaders representing over *one million* people's serving. *Everyone* helped. For fifty-two days, they wholly gave themselves to a single mission: "…for the people had a mind to work" (Nehemiah 4:6). And it was all without remuneration; they were volunteers.

When it comes to teamwork, it takes everyone, and it takes everything. No job is unimportant to a team player. Colossians 3:23–24 commands us, "And whatsoever ye do, do it heartily, as to the Lord, and not unto men; Knowing that of the Lord ye shall receive the reward of the inheritance: for ye serve the Lord Christ."

Leaders should be laborers

The book of Nehemiah gives a sterling picture of servant leadership. Nehemiah not only provided vision, organization, and motivation, but he lived and labored with the people: "Yea, also I continued in the work of this wall…" (Nehemiah 5:16).

Nehemiah's example inspired other leaders to serve. In the list of the names of leaders in the work found in chapter 3, we find mention of several rulers and nobles serving right alongside the common laborers. We even find recorded (by way of dishonorable mention) the one group of nobles who refused to get their hands dirty: "And next unto them the Tekoites repaired; but their nobles put not their necks to the work of their Lord" (Nehemiah 3:5). (How would you like to go down in the pages of Scripture as the leader who refused to serve your Lord? Clearly, God expects leaders to labor.)

Additionally, Nehemiah, who was leading an impoverished people, refused to take advantage of his leadership position, although he well could have: "Moreover from the time that I was appointed to be their governor in the land of Judah, from the twentieth year even unto the two and thirtieth year of Artaxerxes the king, that is, twelve years, I and my brethren have not eaten the bread of the governor....yet for all this required not I the bread of the governor, because the bondage was heavy upon this people" (Nehemiah 5:14, 18).

The servant leadership of Nehemiah and those who led under him is exactly the type of leadership Jesus not only modeled, but instructed us to follow. In Luke 22:27, Jesus rebuked the jockeying-for-position attitude of His disciples with a simple reminder: "For whether is greater, he that sitteth at meat, or he that serveth? is not he that sitteth at meat? but I am among you as he that serveth."

Teamwork makes the dream work

There is no room in the work of the Lord for personality clashes or turf wars. The only way the Jews could complete the massive walls of Jerusalem in just fifty-two days was by setting aside personal differences and laboring together for a common goal.

Some labored as builders and some as burden bearers (Nehemiah 4:17). As the work progressed and outside dangers increased, their cooperation was even more necessary as they took turns on the night watch (Nehemiah 4:21).

Too often in today's world, we weaken the work of God by holding onto grudges, personality differences, or bits of contention. Proverbs 13:10 exposes our differences with one another for what they are: "Only by pride cometh contention: but with the well advised is wisdom." There it is, plain and simple—pride.

One of the best ways to set aside the contentions caused by pride is to humble ourselves, focusing on the reality that the work which has been entrusted to us is much greater than any one person. Paul admonished the church at Philippi: "Only let your conversation be as it becometh the gospel of Christ: that whether I come and see you, or else be absent, I may hear of your affairs, that ye stand fast in one spirit, with one mind striving together for the faith of the gospel" (Philippians 1:27).

Look to the finish line

One of my favorite lines in the book of Nehemiah is found in chapter 6 verse 15: "So the wall was finished...." The teamwork, the effort, the strain, the burdens—it was all for a purpose.

Fifty-two days earlier, there was just a charred pile of rubbish. Fifty-two days later, there were completed walls with gates and towers. And the work was to the glory of God. Even the enemies of God "...perceived that this work was wrought of our God" (Nehemiah 6:16).

Do you need motivation to continue in the work? Do you wonder if you'll ever make it? Look to the one who has already crossed the finish line—look to Jesus!

> ...let us run with patience the race that is set before us, Looking unto Jesus the author and finisher of our faith; who for the joy that was set before him endured the cross, despising the shame, and is set down at the right hand of the throne of God. For consider him...
> —HEBREWS 12:1–3

One of God's kindest gifts to His people is the synergy available through laboring together. If you want to strengthen your hands in the work of the Lord, practice teamwork.

Then said I unto them, Ye see the distress that we are in, how Jerusalem lieth waste, and the gates thereof are burned with fire: come, and let us build up the wall of Jerusalem, that we be no more a reproach.—Nehemiah 2:17

"Never doubt in the night what God gave you in the light."—unknown

Chapter Five
Look beyond the Rubbish

"The explosion was the first warning. The heavy detonation was heard all over West Orange [New Jersey], and every building in the plant was rocked by a giant concussion. Flames leaped at once from all the windows....The walls were cracked by the force of the explosion."[1] So ran the December 10, 1914, *New York Times* front page article describing the destruction of Thomas Edison's plant.

For his part, Edison instructed his adult son, Charles, "Go get your mother and all her friends. They'll never see a fire like this again." When Charles objected, Edison said, "It's all right. We've just got rid of a lot of rubbish."[2]

The "rubbish" was estimated at $7 million (about $23 million today), only $2 million of which was covered by insurance. And yet, Edison positively refused to give in to discouragement. To the *New York Times* reporter, he simply said, "Although I am over sixty-seven years old, I'll start all over again tomorrow. I am pretty well burned out tonight, but tomorrow there will be a mobilization here and the debris will be cleared away, if it is cooled sufficiently, and I will go right to work to reconstruct the plant." In the background, the fire still raged.

How did he do it? How could he watch his life's labor going up in flames and send for his wife to enjoy the spectacle? How could he *in the moment of adversity,* say, "but tomorrow…" finishing his sentence with hope?

The answer is simple. Thomas Edison knew how to work through discouragement.

There is no force in the world that has the potential to weaken your hands like discouragement.

The enemies of Nehemiah knew this. Thus, they called attention, not to the progress on the wall (which was by that point quite substantial), but to the rubbish: "…What do these feeble Jews?…will they revive the stones out of the heaps of the rubbish which are burned?" (Nehemiah 4:2).

And it wasn't just the enemies who saw the rubbish. Even some of the Jews complained, "The strength of the bearers of burdens is decayed, and there is much rubbish; so that we are not able to build the wall" (Nehemiah 4:10). In effect, they said, "We're out of strength, we're not making progress, and we can't do it."

I can identify with these Jews. They were tired, had lost their vision, and felt their strength slipping away. Perhaps you've been there. As a youth pastor, all you can see is the rough kid; as a mom, the unending laundry or the troublesome child; as a spouse, the faults in your mate; as a Christian in any walk of life, the bills, the trials, the burdens, the impossibilities....

The negative is certainly there. What do you do when it's all you can see? How can you find strength when discouragement has gripped your soul?

Nehemiah found the answer: resolutely look beyond the rubbish.

Look to what God can do

When Nehemiah arrived in Jerusalem, all that ordinary eyes could see was rubbish. But where others saw rubbish, Nehemiah saw potential. He knew that God specializes in reviving rubbish.

I have the privilege to serve the Lord in one of the most liberal states in America. California is not only liberal politically, but our state is liberal spiritually as well—so much so that some see California as "the land of fruits and nuts." I don't. I've chosen to see it as the state with the greatest potential for revival.

I don't know where you serve or what obstacles you face, but I do know that if you stare at the obstacles, you will become discouraged. Look instead to what *God* can do. Remember, you serve the God who:

- Created the universe with mere words (Hebrews 11:3).
- Gave Abraham a son (and billions of descendants) when he was "as good as dead" (Hebrews 11:12).
- Parted the Red Sea and provided for an entire nation of people through forty years in the wilderness (Exodus 14; Deuteronomy 8:2–4).
- Gave a shepherd boy victory over a giant, who happened to be a veteran warrior as well (1 Samuel 17).
- Multiplied the meager resources of a starving widow (1 Kings 17:9–16).
- Healed a man with the death sentence of leprosy (2 Kings 5:1–14)
- Protected His servants in the fiery furnace (Daniel 3).

- Sealed the mouths of hungry lions from so much as laying a tooth on His prophet (Daniel 6).
- Delivered Israel from Babylonian captivity (Ezra 1:1–4).
- Raised Christ from the dead (Ephesians 1:18–20).

And "this God is our God" (Psalm 48:14). What's a little rubbish to Him?

Take action

The book of Nehemiah is a record of causative leadership. Nehemiah faced tremendous obstacles, but in each of them, he had a bias for action.

- When he heard the situation was hopeless, he prayed (chapter 1).
- When he needed supplies, he asked (chapter 2).
- When he had an assignment, he organized helpers (chapter 3).
- When the enemies threatened, he armed his workers (chapter 4).
- When disagreements arose, he intervened (chapter 5).
- When critics slandered, he persevered (chapter 6).

And on through the book of Nehemiah. This leader not only saw the walls built, but he saw one of the great revivals of history by calling the people together to hear God's Word. The man knew how to take action when everything around him was falling apart.

When discouragement sets in, it is joined by its cousins, apathy and paralysis. After you lift your eyes from the rubbish to the Lord, do something.

I'm not suggesting that you rush God. After all, Nehemiah's first step on his action plan was prolonged prayer. And prayer *is* something. What I am suggesting is that you refuse to do nothing.

When we're overwhelmed in our spirit, the piles of rubbish loom large and our ability to build something in their place seems feeble. But when we, with our eyes on the power of God, determine to take one step of action, the discouragement begins to dissipate. It often is that first simple action that strengthens our hands for the task.

Rely on the Lord

No matter how sincere or well-directed our steps of action may be, without the intervention of God, we don't stand a chance. Nehemiah knew this; thus, as he challenged the people in their preparedness to fight, he said, "…Be not ye afraid of them: remember the Lord…" (Nehemiah 4:14).

Remember the Lord.

We are weak; He is mighty.

We are unable; He is all-powerful.

We are defenseless; He is our defender.

We are not in it alone! In Isaiah 41:10, God gives these calming words to discouraged hearts: "Fear thou not; for I am with thee: be not dismayed; for I am thy God: I will strengthen thee; yea, I will help thee; yea, I will uphold thee with the right hand of my righteousness."

I am with thee.

For what more could we ask?

What does relying on the Lord look like in practical terms? It means we depend on His promises and walk in His Spirit.

Consider first God's promises. What promise do you need to claim for the piles of rubbish in front of you? Find it. Highlight it in the pages of your Bible. Write it on the walls of your memory. Use it against the giant of discouragement.

But consider, too, the need to walk in the Spirit. We are in a battle, and discouragement is just one of the weapons in Satan's arsenal. "Be sober, be vigilant; because your adversary the devil, as a roaring lion, walketh about, seeking whom he may devour" (1 Peter 5:8). What can we do against such a stealthy, powerful foe? "This I say then, Walk in the Spirit, and ye shall not fulfil the lust of the flesh" (Galatians 5:16). Relying on God's power to defeat our enemy includes submitting to God's Spirit to conquer our own flesh.

Press on

The fifty-two days that it took God's people to rebuild the walls is nothing short of amazing. But remember, it *did* take fifty-two days—days fraught with difficulty, discouragement, threats, fatigue, blisters, taut nerves…. The wall was finished by the power of God through persistent people.

Never underestimate the power of persistence. Discouragement rarely knocks once and leaves. As long as there is rubbish present, you and I will be tempted to focus our attention on the rubbish. Don't. Refuse.

Instead, look to what God can do, take action, and rely on the Lord. And then repeat. Press on until the rubbish is cleared, the harvest is ended, and we see our Lord face to face.

And let us not be weary in well doing: for in due season we shall reap, if we faint not.
—GALATIANS 6:9

1. *New York Times* (December 10, 1914), http://query.nytimes.com/mem/archive-free/pdf?res=9B0CE5DE1438E633A25753C1A9649D946596D6CF, (accessed 21 May 2015).

2. Richard Feloni, *Business Insider* (May 9, 2014), http://www.businessinsider.com/thomas-edison-in-the-obstacle-is-the-way-2014-5, (accessed 21 May 2015).

Chapter Six
Persist through Opposition

One of my more naive thoughts as I entered the ministry was that everyone would be happy to see any forward progress made for God. That was before I met Mike.

Mike was addicted to drugs when I had the privilege of sharing the gospel with him. He was at an all-time low with his addiction spiraling out of control and his life unraveling with it. His wife had left him and taken the children, partly for physical safety and partly for her sanity. His finances and his credit were blown.

And then Mike got saved, and everything about his life changed. The Lord changed him inside and out. Mike was faithful in church and eager in growth. In time and after counseling, the Lord even healed his marriage. Soon, he and his wife were growing together—soaking in God's Word, coming to every church service, tithing, serving, and teaching their children the things of God.

There was, however, a surprising side effect to Mike's transformation. His parents were angry. They weren't just a little angry either. They were *very* angry—with Mike, with me, with Christianity. And they expressed their displeasure in no uncertain terms.

I never could understand it. While Mike was pouring money down the drain through drugs, abusing his wife, and ruining his life, his parents loved and "supported" him. But when his life was back on track, his marriage healed, and his family happy, they thought he had lost his mind. Their reasons were surface—he was at church too much, shouldn't give money to the church, etc. But none of it made sense to me. Sometimes it seemed to me that they actually would have preferred if he was living his old lifestyle.

Obviously, not every dramatic life change has such complicated ramifications, but Mike's growth and his parents' response woke me up to the serious realities of spiritual warfare. The truth is, no Christian victories are celebrated by everyone. Even in the cases when every person immediately involved rejoices, Satan seethes.

In Nehemiah's case, he wasn't even building the wall for himself. Truth be told, he would have had a more comfortable life back at his secure government job in the palace. The burden of leadership and labor was one he assumed purely voluntarily (in response to the call of God and opportunities opened through prayer) with godly, generous motives. Yet, he still encountered opposition.

With every wave of victory came a renewed wave of opposition. From the beginning of Nehemiah's efforts to rebuild the wall, the enemies of God were grieved: "When Sanballat the Horonite, and Tobiah the servant, the Ammonite, heard of it, it grieved them exceedingly that there was come a man to seek the welfare of the children of Israel" (Nehemiah 2:10). And it was downhill from there.

> But it came to pass, that when Sanballat heard that we builded the wall, he was wroth, and took great indignation, and mocked the Jews. And he spake before his brethren and the army of Samaria, and said, What do these feeble Jews? will they fortify themselves? will they sacrifice? will they make an end in a day? will they revive

the stones out of the heaps of the rubbish which
are burned? Now Tobiah the Ammonite was by
him, and he said, Even that which they build, if
a fox go up, he shall even break down their stone
wall.—NEHEMIAH 4:1–3

This opposition was real. Anger and jealousy spewed
out in mocking sarcasm. His critics questioned his motives,
his abilities, and the viability of the project itself. As
progress on the wall continued, what had begun as stinging
ridicule escalated into direct threat.

But it came to pass, that when Sanballat, and
Tobiah, and the Arabians, and the Ammonites,
and the Ashdodites, heard that the walls of
Jerusalem were made up, and that the breaches
began to be stopped, then they were very wroth,
And conspired all of them together to come
and to fight against Jerusalem, and to hinder it.
—NEHEMIAH 4:7–8

Every godly Christian will face opposition.
Second Timothy 3:12 says it in unequivocal terms:
"Yea, and all that will live godly in Christ Jesus shall
suffer persecution."

Direct physical persecution may not be widespread in America today (although it is higher than ever before in the rest of the world), but there is mounting anger, cynicism, and intolerance even here in the United States toward Christians. And as if that weren't enough, distracted Christians are notorious for their own friendly fire issues that result in spiritual casualties and losses to the cause of Christ, all the more tragic because of their source.

So what do you do when you encounter opposition? How do you strengthen your hands for the work when there are others actively working to weaken your hands and cut off your influence or ability?

Remember to whom you answer

Sanballat made a grave mistake in his mockery of the Jews' efforts. In his suggestion that even a fox could "break down their stone wall," it is obvious that he didn't realize whom he was opposing. The wall wasn't "theirs"; it was God's. Nehemiah was the superintendent, but God was the designer.

The world doesn't understand that our mission is heavenly, that the church itself isn't even man's invention but Christ's. Jesus declared, "…upon this rock I will build my church; and the gates of hell shall not prevail against it" (Matthew 16:18).

When you are criticized, slandered, or mocked for the cause of Christ, remember that you don't answer to your critic; you answer to the Lord. Like Nehemiah, you can simply ignore the criticism. And, like Christ instructed and first-century Christians practiced, you can take it a step further and "Rejoice, and be exceeding glad: for great is your reward in heaven: for so persecuted they the prophets which were before you" (Matthew 5:12).

Pray

By chapter 4 of Nehemiah, it comes as no surprise that Nehemiah's immediate response to criticism was prayer.

Directly following both mentions of opposition recorded above is a record of Nehemiah's prayer:

> Hear, O our God; for we are despised: and turn their reproach upon their own head, and give them for a prey in the land of captivity:
> —NEHEMIAH 4:4

> Nevertheless we made our prayer unto our God, and set a watch against them day and night, because of them.—NEHEMIAH 4:9

God desires to use the pressure of opposition to teach us the power of prayer. Too often, however, we neglect prayer, running first to our own defense. In doing so, we discard the opportunity to release our burdens to the power of God, to take advantage of the invitation given in 1 Peter 5:7: "Casting all your care upon him; for he careth for you."

James 5:13 invites, "Is any among you afflicted? let him pray...." Surely *affliction* includes the troubles imposed by opposition and persecution. The passage further confirms what Nehemiah's testimony demonstrates, "The effectual fervent prayer of a righteous man availeth much" (James 5:16).

Continue building

An unknown author commented, "The best way to answer a critic is to accomplish your task." Nehemiah seemed to be of the same opinion, for after prayer, he simply persisted in the work: "So built we the wall; and all the wall was joined together unto the half thereof: for the people had a mind to work" (Nehemiah 4:6).

One of Satan's goals in sending opposition our way is to sidetrack us. It makes no difference to him if the opposition is successful through direct attack or through sidetracking our focus. In either case, the result is the same.

Don't let Satan gain this advantage. Are you being criticized? Ridiculed? Scorned? Continue building the areas you are called to lead—your home, Sunday school class, ministry, church. Keep serving your Saviour. "Therefore, my beloved brethren, be ye stedfast, unmoveable, always abounding in the work of the Lord, forasmuch as ye know that your labour is not in vain in the Lord" (1 Corinthians 15:58).

Watch

When Sanballat and his cronies issued a physical threat, Nehemiah put feet to his prayers: "Nevertheless we made our prayer unto our God, and set a watch against them day and night, because of them" (Nehemiah 4:9). The rest of the chapter details how extensive this defense was, how Nehemiah worked to keep the workers encouraged in spite of it, and how the people kept building through it.

Christian casualties are real, and we cannot afford to let our guard down even when—no, *especially* when—we are seeing progress and blessing in our labor. For these are the times Satan is most likely to attack us.

Jesus instructed His disciples, "Watch and pray, that ye enter not into temptation: the spirit indeed is willing, but the flesh is weak" (Matthew 26:41). The apostle Paul reinforced, "Watch ye, stand fast in the faith, quit you like men, be strong" (1 Corinthians 16:13).

God has given us the full armor we need for spiritual warfare, but we must not neglect to use it: "Wherefore take unto you the whole armour of God, that ye may be able to withstand in the evil day, and having done all, to stand" (Ephesians 6:13).

Take courage

Anything going forward faces opposition. Our tendency is to see opposition as a sign of defeat, but in reality it may be a sign of progress.

The opposition you face may outwardly look different than Nehemiah's. Yet, like Nehemiah's opponents, there is a deeper source for opposition we encounter in the work of the Lord—spiritual warfare. And we already know, "…greater is he that is in you, than he that is in the world" (1 John 4:4).

So take courage! And keep building.

And I sent messengers unto them, saying, I am doing a great work, so that I cannot come down: why should the work cease, whilst I leave it, and come down to you?—Nehemiah 6:3

"The men who have moved the world have been the men whom the world could not move."—unknown

Chapter Seven
Refuse To Compromise

A hunter raised his rifle and took careful aim at a large bear. When he was about to pull the trigger, the bear spoke in a soft soothing voice, "Isn't it better to talk than to shoot? What do you want? Let's negotiate the matter."

Lowering his rifle, the hunter replied, "I want a fur coat."

"Good," said the bear, "that is a negotiable question. I only want a full stomach, so let us work out a compromise."

They sat down to negotiate and after a time the bear walked away alone. The negotiations had been successful.

The bear had a full stomach, and the hunter had his fur coat.

When those who do not share your goals—namely, God's glory through the building of His work—want to negotiate, the result is bound to parallel that of the hunter and the bear. It was this vein of negotiations that Sanballat and Tobiah sought with Nehemiah.

> Now it came to pass, when Sanballat, and Tobiah, and Geshem the Arabian, and the rest of our enemies, heard that I had built the wall, and that there was no breach left therein; (though at that time I had not set up the doors upon the gates;) That Sanballat and Geshem sent unto me, saying, Come, let us meet together in some one of the villages in the plain of Ono. But they thought to do me mischief.—NEHEMIAH 6:1–2

Remember, Nehemiah had experienced great challenges already. By God's grace, he had remained strong, and the work on the wall was progressing. In fact, at the beginning of Nehemiah 6, the wall is nearly complete. By this time, Nehemiah was surely feeling the strain of relentless opposition. An offer to simply talk things out could have been welcome. But Nehemiah was wiser than that. His response is legendary: "I am doing a great work, so that I cannot come down" (Nehemiah 6:3).

Although compromise may have seemed that it would provide relief in the moment, in the long run, it would have weakened the workers and destroyed the work.

Sanballat, however, didn't easily take "no" for an answer: "Yet they sent unto me four times after this sort." But Nehemiah remained resolute: "and I answered them after the same manner" (Nehemiah 6:4).

Eventually, the enemies increased their efforts to open slander and direct threats, which we'll see in a moment. Still, Nehemiah stood.

Satan's attack on God's work through compromise didn't dissolve when Nehemiah finished the wall. He actively and aggressively seeks to make deals with God's people today. And the deals are never good for God's work. Whether his offer is an invitation to compromise our commitment, doctrine, biblical philosophy and methods, or separation and holiness, our answer must echo Nehemiah's: "No."

How did Nehemiah have the wisdom to discern the true nature of these intentions and the strength to maintain the integrity of the work? And how can you and I resist temptations to compromise?

Use discernment

Sanballat and Geshem's offer was to meet in a quiet village in the plain of Ono, some thirty miles northwest of Jerusalem. It is a beautiful area and could have provided a restful break for Nehemiah—a mini personal retreat.

But somehow, Nehemiah had an intuition that this offer was not all that it seemed. Perhaps it was the previous threats of Sanballat that gave Nehemiah a clue. Even so, it would have been easy to convince himself things had changed. But Nehemiah was more discerning than that. His commentary on the offer was simple: "But they thought to do me mischief." Whether their goal was to abduct or murder him is not clear, but neither would have been a happy compromise for Nehemiah or the work of God.

Reading this story in hindsight, it's easy to see that a trap was being set. But Christians today fall for similar enticements. Discouraged and weary of labor, they listen to those who would draw them to compromise doctrinal or personal integrity.

We can learn a lesson from Nehemiah. Those who blatantly attack the work of God only offer compromises that are in their favor—no matter how peacefully they word their offers. We need to exercise discernment today to avoid both apostasy and compromise.

> Beloved, believe not every spirit, but try the spirits whether they are of God: because many false prophets are gone out into the world. —1 JOHN 4:1

> And this I pray, that your love may abound yet more and more in knowledge and in all judgment; That ye may approve things that are excellent; that ye may be sincere and without offence till the day of Christ;—PHILIPPIANS 1:9–10

Recognize the value of your work

Nehemiah gave two simple reasons for rejecting the offer of compromise: 1) I am doing a great work. 2) The work would cease if I come down.

> And I sent messengers unto them, saying, I am doing a great work, so that I cannot come down: why should the work cease, whilst I leave it, and come down to you?—NEHEMIAH 6:3

One of Satan's ploys in bringing us to consider his offers of compromise is to cause us to question the importance of our work. He may draw our attention to others who are experiencing great financial or worldly success. He may draw our attention to our failures or even to what is incomplete and label it a failure.

But when we are involved in the work of God, especially as we are obeying the Great Commission of Christ by taking the gospel to others, we are invested in a great work indeed. It is a work with eternal fruit. Likewise, if we neglect it, the consequences are eternal.

When you are tempted to compromise, ask yourself two questions: "What is my estimation of the work of God? Is God's work as important as this offered relief?"

Whether you are a mother raising children for God, a pastor reaching a community for Christ, a Sunday school teacher nurturing spiritual growth in hearts, or a leader in any other capacity seeking to make a difference in the work of God, recognize the value of your labor. And remind yourself of it when you are tempted to compromise.

Respond with truth

With his offers for a meeting spurned, Sanballat launched a new campaign to stop Nehemiah's labor. It was multifaceted, but he launched it with an open letter.

You've read open letters, perhaps circulated on the Internet or copied to a large group through email. They're seldom kind and are often slanderous. They are intended to put someone on the spot and force a public response. In Sanballat's letter, he accused Nehemiah of a planned rebellion and of seeking to make himself a king. He based it on nebulous sources ("It is reported") and made ridiculous leaps of logic. And, of course, he ended it with an easy out for Nehemiah—*let's talk.*

> Then sent Sanballat his servant unto me in like manner the fifth time with an open letter in his hand; Wherein was written, It is reported among the heathen, and Gashmu saith it, that thou and the Jews think to rebel: for which cause thou buildest the wall, that thou mayest be their king, according to these words. And thou hast also appointed prophets to preach of thee at Jerusalem, saying, There is a king in Judah: and now shall it be reported to the king according to these words. Come now therefore, and let us take counsel together.—NEHEMIAH 6:5–7

Nehemiah was wiser than to engage the enemy in a public forum. He gave a brief, curt response and (not surprisingly) turned to the Lord in prayer.

> Then I sent unto him, saying, There are no such things done as thou sayest, but thou

feignest them out of thine own heart. For they
all made us afraid, saying, Their hands shall be
weakened from the work, that it be not done.
Now therefore, O God, strengthen my hands.
—NEHEMIAH 6:8–9

Satan is a master at twisting truth and engaging doubt.
You and I are not smart enough, wise enough, or strong
enough to enter mental combat with him. Our best—
indeed, our only—recourse is truth.

And take…the sword of the Spirit, which is the
word of God: Praying always with all prayer
and supplication in the Spirit, and watching
thereunto with all perseverance and supplication
for all saints;—EPHESIANS 6:17–18

When confusion sets in, use God's Word as a
weapon, and cry out to God in prayer. These resources
will strengthen your hands against the temptation
to compromise.

Reject fear

When the open letter fell flat, Sanballat worked undercover,
hiring someone to work as a fear monger.

Afterward I came unto the house of Shemaiah the son of Delaiah the son of Mehetabeel, who was shut up; and he said, Let us meet together in the house of God, within the temple, and let us shut the doors of the temple: for they will come to slay thee; yea, in the night will they come to slay thee. And I said, Should such a man as I flee? and who is there, that, being as I am, would go into the temple to save his life? I will not go in. And, lo, I perceived that God had not sent him; but that he pronounced this prophecy against me: for Tobiah and Sanballat had hired him. Therefore was he hired, that I should be afraid, and do so, and sin, and that they might have matter for an evil report, that they might reproach me.—NEHEMIAH 6:10–13

Once again, we see the perception of Nehemiah. Discerning the true intentions of Shemaiah, Nehemiah flatly refused to be controlled by fear. The tougher the battle, the greater his dependence upon God.

Fear has the power to weaken us like few other forces. No wonder Scripture so often repeats the phrase, "Fear not."

Be strong and of a good courage, fear not, nor be afraid of them: for the LORD thy God, he it is that doth go with thee; he will not fail thee, nor forsake thee.—DEUTERONOMY 31:6

And the LORD, he it is that doth go before thee; he will be with thee, he will not fail thee, neither forsake thee: fear not, neither be dismayed. —DEUTERONOMY 31:8

And Joshua said unto them, Fear not, nor be dismayed, be strong and of good courage: for thus shall the LORD do to all your enemies against whom ye fight.—JOSHUA 10:25

And he answered, Fear not: for they that be with us are more than they that be with them. —2 KINGS 6:16

For I the LORD thy God will hold thy right hand, saying unto thee, Fear not; I will help thee. —ISAIAH 41:13

But now thus saith the LORD that created thee, O Jacob, and he that formed thee, O Israel, Fear not: for I have redeemed thee, I have called thee by thy name; thou art mine.—ISAIAH 43:1

But even the very hairs of your head are all numbered. Fear not therefore: ye are of more value than many sparrows.—LUKE 12:7

And that's just a sampling!

When we reject fear, clinging to the promises of God's presence, we are free to persevere in the work of God.

So the wall was finished

Thanks to Nehemiah's steadfast refusal to compromise, before chapter 6 ends, it records simply, "So the wall was finished."

Had Nehemiah caved to the pressure of Sanballat, this story would have had a different ending. But he didn't. He built the wall and restored national dignity because he would not quit, compromise, or pursue trivial matters.

Are you facing temptations to compromise? Don't let down your guard. As God prospers your labors, Satan will try new angles in his attacks. The stakes of compromise are always higher than they appear. Accept the offers to compromise, and you weaken your hands. Determine "I cannot come down," and strengthen your hands.

And all the people gathered themselves together as one man into the street that was before the water gate; and they spake unto Ezra the scribe to bring the book of the law of Moses, which the LORD had commanded to Israel.—Nehemiah 8:1

"Now what is food for the inner man? Not prayer, but the Word of God; and here again, not the simple reading of the Word of God, so that it only passes through our minds, just as water passes through a pipe, but considering what we read, pondering it over and applying it to our hearts."—George Müller

Chapter Eight
Anchor Your Hope in God's Word

We are living in a day when Americans seem to think that the answers to our problems always lie in a new program or, if not a program, another person in leadership. I appreciate a helpful program as much as the next person, and I'm all for having wise leaders in positions to address problems. But the fact is, neither programs nor people can provide the help we need at deepest levels of the soul—where we most need help.

Throughout the book of Nehemiah, we see this godly leader's dependence on the Word of God. From the very first chapter, when Nehemiah stated his case in prayer with God's Word, to chapter 8, when God's Word brought a great revival, we are reminded that Scripture is the foundation for our hope. It has the power to strengthen our hands personally and create real change corporately.

To understand the outpouring of the revival in Nehemiah 8—one of the first revivals of all time—consider the background. By this point, the wall had been finished, people had settled into housing areas throughout the city, and government had been established. In spite of these advancements, however, Nehemiah sensed a spiritual vacuum.

And so it is today. Programs and prosperity mean nothing without God's power. As leaders, sometimes it is easy for us to invest only in building measurable programs. But God not only builds walls; He builds people. Our goals are not only numeric; they are spiritual.

How do we strengthen our hands in the delicate, but needful, work of building hearts and of seeing personal and corporate revival? The answer is as broad as it is simple— God's Word. Scripture must be our tool in the work as well as our sustenance for the work.

What does that mean in practical terms? Let's answer that question from Nehemiah 8.

Expose your heart to Scripture

This may sound obvious, but to draw strength from God's Word, we must expose ourselves to it. It doesn't soak into our spirits by osmosis, and it doesn't strengthen our hands by mere knowledge. We must open our hearts to it.

On a personal level, this means spending time in God's Word daily. Remember, the Bible gives perspective and promise like no other source. It gives direction and wisdom. Time with the Lord in His Word settles our spirits and realigns our focus.

Yet, somehow, Christian leaders all too easily neglect this vital spiritual discipline. Don't. We neglect Scripture at our own peril and to our own weakness. "Every word of God is pure: he is a shield unto them that put their trust in him" (Proverbs 30:5). Wouldn't it make sense, then, that we read, study, and love God's Word? There is no substitute for it.

On a corporate level, this means following God's instruction to assemble as a church and expose our hearts to the preaching of His Word. Hebrews 10:25 cautions, "Not forsaking the assembling of ourselves together, as the manner of some is; but exhorting one another: and so much the more, as ye see the day approaching."

This corporate exposure is what we see in Nehemiah 8:

> And all the people gathered themselves together
> as one man into the street that was before the
> water gate; and they spake unto Ezra the scribe
> to bring the book of the law of Moses, which the
> LORD had commanded to Israel.—NEHEMIAH 8:1

Listen to God's voice

The old French proverb, "A good meal ought to begin with hunger," is true in both the physical and the spiritual sense. If we don't have a hunger for God's Word, we won't appreciate and apply it as we should. How easily we let it go in one ear and out the other with no hunger to hear God's voice, no inclining our ears to catch the still small voice of the Holy Spirit!

The Jews in Nehemiah's day not only assembled to hear God's Word, but they actually requested to hear it, and they listened attentively—for a long period of time!

> ...they spake unto Ezra the scribe to bring
> the book of the law of Moses...And he read
> therein before the street that was before the
> water gate from the morning until midday,
> before the men and the women, and those
> that could understand; and the ears of all the

people were attentive unto the book of the law.
—Nehemiah 8:1, 3

The moments of conviction, courage, and strength don't come from God's Word if our bodies are physically present but our thoughts are far away. May our hearts instead echo the cries of the psalmist: "Behold, I have longed after thy precepts:…And I will delight myself in thy commandments, which I have loved" (Psalm 119:40, 47).

Use Scripture in ministry

The revival in Nehemiah 8 would never have happened had the Jews assembled to hear God's Word, but had only been entertained—perhaps with music, perhaps with a recounting of the walls' being built. God-honoring music and testimonies of victory are wonderful, but only the Word of God has the power to bring about revival. Hebrews 4:12 says, "For the word of God is quick, and powerful, and sharper than any twoedged sword, piercing even to the dividing asunder of soul and spirit, and of the joints and marrow, and is a discerner of the thoughts and intents of the heart."

Use this powerful tool in ministry. Use it in witnessing, preaching, teaching, counseling, and any other time you want to reach hearts with truth. Saturate your ministry with Scripture. Take time to explain the meaning of passages and to help apply them to lives. This is the job of a spiritual leader—connecting God's Word to the hearts of hearers.

> So they read in the book in the law of God distinctly, and gave the sense, and caused them to understand the reading.—NEHEMIAH 8:8

Respond to the Word of God

The story of the revival in Nehemiah 8 begins with attentively hearing God's Word, but it ends in a dramatic response to Scripture that continued throughout the next chapters.

The people didn't simply *hear* God's Word; they *obeyed* God's Word. They responded. Likewise, if we intend to benefit from the strengthening power of God's Word, we will hear and respond.

> But be ye doers of the word, and not hearers only, deceiving your own selves. For if any be a hearer of the word, and not a doer, he is like unto a man beholding his natural face in a glass: For he beholdeth himself, and goeth his way, and

straightway forgetteth what manner of man he was. But whoso looketh into the perfect law of liberty, and continueth therein, he being not a forgetful hearer, but a doer of the work, this man shall be blessed in his deed.—JAMES 1:22–25

It is only as we respond to the Word of God that we find it transforming our lives and strengthening us for the work God has called us to do. And it is only as we invite others to respond that we see its transforming power in their lives.

Then he said unto them, Go your way, eat the fat, and drink the sweet, and send portions unto them for whom nothing is prepared: for this day is holy unto our Lord: neither be ye sorry; for the joy of the LORD is your strength. —Nehemiah 8:10

"The Lord gives His people perpetual joy when they walk in obedience to Him." —D. L. Moody

Chapter Nine
Find Your Joy in the Lord

It was Easter morning, 1799, in the small town of Feldkirch, Austria, when the armies of Napoleon appeared. Aware that they had no means of defending themselves, the town council called a hasty meeting and prepared to surrender.

After much discussion, the dean of the church rose and said, "My brothers it is Easter Day! We have been reckoning our own strength, and that fails. Let us turn to God. Ring the bells and have service as usual, and leave the matter in God's hands."

The council agreed, and joyous peals rang from the church bells as worshippers filled the streets hastening to service.

The French heard the sudden ringing of the joy bells with surprise and alarm. Concluding that the Austrian army had arrived to defend the town, they fled. Before the bells had ceased ringing, not a Frenchman was to be seen.[1]

In the midst of spiritual warfare today, many Christians falter and give up in defeat. Some would ask, "Where is our strength?" But I believe the real question is, "Where is our joy?" For, as Nehemiah commented, "the joy of the Lord is your strength" (Nehemiah 8:10).

Joy is an inner resource of the child of God that provides hidden strength for the onslaught of Satan's attacks. And Satan does attack. He constantly works to rob us of our joy. Through personal trials, ministry burdens, life difficulties, and circumstances outside our control, his goal is to undermine our strength and deplete our hope.

Without the joy of the Lord, we are more vulnerable to Satan's attacks. With it, our hands are strong to labor.

So how do we experience this joy? In the intensity of spiritual battle and the pressures of leadership, where do we find the joy of the Lord?

Remember your salvation

Nehemiah's statement on the joy of the Lord was to a revival-renewed people who had just heard and understood God's Word: "And all the people went their way to eat, and to drink, and to send portions, and to make great mirth, because they had understood the words that were declared unto them" (Nehemiah 8:12).

The greatest moment of life is when we hear and understand what God's Word says about the payment Christ made for our sin. When we place our faith in Him as our Saviour, we have true cause for continuous joy.

The Jews in Nehemiah's day wept as their sin was exposed through God's Word. We who know Christ as our Saviour find in God's Word that we are covered with His righteousness: "I will greatly rejoice in the LORD, my soul shall be joyful in my God; for he hath clothed me with the garments of salvation, he hath covered me with the robe of righteousness, as a bridegroom decketh himself with ornaments, and as a bride adorneth herself with her jewels" (Isaiah 61:10).

Do you remember the moment you were saved? Do you remember the joy of receiving the gift of eternal life (Romans 6:23) and resting in the promise of God (Romans 10:13)? The truth is, even at that time there were problems in your life. (You may have even realized your need for Christ *because* of those problems.) But at the moment of salvation, your heart was focused on Christ and overflowing with joy.

Regardless of what difficulties you face today, you can rejoice in the fact that you are saved. Habakkuk 3:18 says, "Yet I will rejoice in the LORD, I will joy in the God of my salvation." That choice to rejoice in your salvation gives strength.

Abide in Christ

Spiritual leaders desire strength for their areas of service. But strength for what we do comes from strength in who Christ is. It is by abiding in Him—daily walking in fellowship with Him—that we have a continuous source of strength. Jesus used the analogy of a branch drawing nourishment from the vine: "Abide in me, and I in you. As the branch cannot bear fruit of itself, except it abide in the vine; no more can ye, except ye abide in me. I am the vine, ye are the branches: He that abideth in me, and I in him, the same bringeth forth much fruit: for without me ye can do nothing" (John 15:4–5).

Abiding in fellowship with Christ includes regular intake of the Word of God. The prophet Jeremiah found "joy and rejoicing" through the words of God: "Thy words were found, and I did eat them; and thy word was unto me the joy and rejoicing of mine heart: for I am called by thy name, O Lord God of hosts" (Jeremiah 15:16).

The natural result of an abiding relationship with Christ is joy. In the same conversation when Jesus told His disciples to abide in Him, He further explained, "These things have I spoken unto you, that my joy might remain in you, and that your joy might be full" (John 15:11).

Serve the Lord

Although serving can be exhausting, God replenishes our strength as we serve; and service itself brings its own reward. Nehemiah knew this better than anyone. He labored night and day and hit more obstacles than he had ever imagined in the process. Yet with the walls completed and the people of God experiencing revival, this otherwise-weary leader could say, "The joy of the Lord is your strength."

In the words of Psalm 100:2, "Serve the Lord with gladness…." He is worthy of our service, and He refills our joy as we serve.

There is a caveat I should mention to the joy found in serving. This joy comes as we serve *the Lord.* In truth, we serve God by serving others. If we serve others expecting our joy to come from them or from their recognition and thanks, we're setting ourselves up for disappointment and, eventually, resentment. But if we serve others for the sake of the Lord, looking to Him for our reward, we can serve with full joy even when our labor goes unnoticed or unthanked by those we serve. "For God is not unrighteous to forget your work and labour of love, which ye have shewed toward his name, in that ye have ministered to the saints, and do minister" (Hebrews 6:10).

Share the gospel

Next to the joy of salvation itself is the joy of leading another person to Christ. This joy is referenced often throughout Scripture.

Psalm 126:6 tells us, "He that goeth forth and weepeth, bearing precious seed, shall doubtless come again with rejoicing, bringing his sheaves with him."

Jesus compared a lost soul's salvation to the joy a shepherd feels when a lost sheep is found: "And when he hath found it, he layeth it on his shoulders, rejoicing. And when he cometh home, he calleth together his friends and neighbours, saying unto them, Rejoice with me; for I have found my sheep which was lost" (Luke 15:5–6). Furthermore, He said, "Likewise, I say unto you, there is joy in the presence of the angels of God over one sinner that repenteth" (Luke 15:10).

Acts 8 records Philip preaching the gospel in Samaria with many people trusting Christ. Verse 8 summarizes, "And there was great joy in that city."

When a person trusts Christ as his Saviour, there is joy all the way around—joy in Heaven, joy in the new Christian's heart, and joy for the one who led him to Christ.

Maintain an eternal perspective

One day, every burden of labor and leadership will vanish, and we will step into eternity. On that day, and for all eternity after, we will bask in the presence of the Lord.

Until that day, remember that "our light affliction, which is but for a moment, worketh for us a far more exceeding and eternal weight of glory; While we look not at the things which are seen, but at the things which are not seen: for the things which are seen are temporal; but the things which are not seen are eternal" (2 Corinthians 4:17–18).

It's true that we endure suffering here that brings tears and heartache. But, it is also true that "the sufferings of this present time are not worthy to be compared with the glory which shall be revealed in us" (Romans 8:18). And as we remember this truth, we can experience the joy of the Lord even in suffering.

Rejoice in the Lord

To the suffering believers at Philippi, Paul wrote, "Rejoice in the Lord alway: and again I say, Rejoice" (Philippians 4:4). Our circumstances fluctuate, but our God never changes. "Jesus Christ the same yesterday, and to day, and for ever" (Hebrews 13:8).

When we pin our joy to prosperity, victory, or progress, we will find our strength ebbing away during downturns. But when we pin our joy to God Himself, making a deliberate decision to rejoice *in Him,* we will find unending reasons to rejoice. And, as a bonus, we will find that this joy becomes our strength.

---

1.   Walter Baxendale, *Dictionary of Anecdote, Incident, Illustrative Fact* (Thomas Whittaker, 1988), 190.

Also that day they offered great sacrifices, and rejoiced: for God had made them rejoice with great joy: the wives also and the children rejoiced: so that the joy of Jerusalem was heard even afar off.—Nehemiah 12:43

"When we bless God for mercies, we usually prolong them. When we bless God for miseries, we usually end them."—Charles H. Spurgeon

Chapter Ten
Give Thanks

Terrie's and my first Thanksgiving together was sure to be slim. I was a nineteen-year-old Bible college student, and I wasn't exactly what you would call wealthy. At the time, I worked for Shepherd Marketing in City of Industry, California. I was thankful for my job with their Caterpillar Tractor dealership and grateful for the opportunity it gave me to provide for my new bride.

About a week before Thanksgiving, Jim Anderson, the General Manager, gave every employee a small cornish hen. I could hardly believe his generosity—this few pound bird would mean that Terrie and I would have a Thanksgiving dinner.

My amazement was compounded, however, when I heard the older guys at work complain about the size of the gift. "What does Jim think we're going to do with a bird this little anyway?" "He's cheap—he just gives us this game hen to make us like him."

I took the game hen home, and Terrie baked it. I also wrote a thank you note to Mr. Anderson. It was pretty simple—I just thanked him for his thoughtfulness and let him know I appreciated my job. I sent the note; we ate the hen; and that was the end of the story in my mind.

A few days later, I was shocked to see Jim Anderson approach me on the loading docks at work. He had asked his secretary to look up where I worked and then asked someone to point me out. He walked over and shook my hand. "Paul," he said, "over all the years I have given company employees a turkey for Thanksgiving, you are the only one who has ever written me a thank you note. I just want you to know that I appreciate that."

I had no idea that one simple note of thanks would mean so much to this manager of a prestigious company that he found time to seek out a nineteen-year-old laborer to tell him so.

God delights to hear our thanks as well. In fact, Psalm 22:3 says, "But thou art holy, O thou that inhabitest the praises of Israel."

As the book of Nehemiah comes to a close, God's people are holding a service of thanksgiving as they dedicate the wall and praise God for giving them the ability to complete it.

Praise and thanksgiving allow us to render gratitude to God for His mercies. They also remind us of the goodness of God and thus strengthen our faith. In Nehemiah 12, we find four ways to express our thanks to God.

Praise the Lord in song

The thanks of God's people welled up in great hymns of gratitude.

> And at the dedication of the wall of Jerusalem they sought the Levites out of all their places, to bring them to Jerusalem, to keep the dedication with gladness, both with thanksgivings, and with singing, with cymbals, psalteries, and with harps. And the sons of the singers gathered themselves together, both out of the plain country round

about Jerusalem, and from the villages of
Netophathi; Also from the house of Gilgal, and
out of the fields of Geba and Azmaveth: for the
singers had builded them villages round about
Jerusalem…—NEHEMIAH 12:27–29

Further in the chapter, verse 43 records that "the joy
of Jerusalem was heard even afar off."

One of the great purposes of God's gift of music is
to give thanks to Him. Throughout Scripture, especially in
Psalms, we see God's people praising the Lord in song.

Perhaps one of the most convicting of these records
occurs in Acts 16. Paul and Silas had seen much fruit in the
city of Philippi as they preached the gospel. Persecution
followed to the extent that these missionaries were
publicly whipped and then cast into the "inner prison"—
the dungeon—with their feet held in stocks. Yet verse 25
records, "And at midnight Paul and Silas prayed, and sang
praises unto God: and the prisoners heard them."

So sing your thanks to God when your heart
overflows with gratitude, and sing your thanks when
it's midnight in your soul. In either circumstance, God
delights to hear your praise, and your hands will be
strengthened by offering it.

Give thanks from a pure heart

Those who led the praise of God's people took care that their offering of praise was not only from their lips but also from their hearts: "And the priests and the Levites purified themselves…" (Nehemiah 12:30).

The old maxim, "Holiness precedes happiness," is absolutely true. Matthew 5:8 says, "Blessed are the pure in heart: for they shall see God."

God is not glorified and we are not strengthened when we praise God out of hypocritical hearts. So give thanks from a pure heart.

Express gratitude through giving

In this celebration of thanks, the people wanted their spirit of thanksgiving to be not a mere moment of ecstasy, but an ongoing matter of worship. They gave monetary gifts to the Lord and set up treasurers and chambers to continue receiving their tithes and offerings.

> And at that time were some appointed over the chambers for the treasures, for the offerings, for the firstfruits, and for the tithes, to gather into them out of the fields of the cities the portions of the law for the priests and Levites: for Judah

rejoiced for the priests and for the Levites that
waited.—NEHEMIAH 12:44

An ungrateful heart finds it difficult to give. But when
we recognize that God is the source of all our blessings
and when our hearts are stirred in gratitude toward Him,
we will desire to give—to the Lord, to His work, and to
His people.

Offer the sacrifice of praise

One of the most humbling testimonies of gratitude is that
of the pilgrims. Few Americans have had more setbacks in
their lives than the group that arrived at Plymouth Rock
in 1620. History tells us that in the first year, the pilgrims
made seven times as many graves than huts. Yet, at the end
of the year, they set aside three full days for giving thanks.

I don't believe that first thanksgiving was the result
only of a bountiful harvest. I believe it was the glad offering
of people who had truly grateful hearts all year long and
were glad for the provision to celebrate their gratitude.

No matter what trials beset you, could I encourage
you? Give thanks. It will honor your God and strengthen
your hands.

By him therefore let us offer the sacrifice of praise to God continually, that is, the fruit of our lips giving thanks to his name.—HEBREWS 13:15

Conclusion
Keep Building

One of the defining moments in my life occurred at a restaurant table nearly thirty years ago. Across the table was a man who had been one of my childhood heroes. Years earlier, he had preached in our church and signed my Bible.

So, when he called me to tell me he would be in the area and would like to take me to lunch, I was thrilled. I could hardly wait to tell him what God was doing in our ministry and to ask him questions. I pictured a mentoring-type of conversation, and I was humbled that he wanted to make himself available to me.

To my great disappointment, he didn't bring up spiritual topics at all. In fact, within a few minutes, I learned that he was out of the ministry and had actually taken me to lunch because he wanted to sell me life insurance! In those moments, I quietly resolved in my heart to finish my life doing what God called me to do from the beginning.

Too many Christian leaders begin their course with joy, excitement, and enthusiasm. But as life happens, burdens pile, and temptations come, these leaders find their strength waning and their commitment fizzling.

Nehemiah was a leader who not only started well, but he finished well. In fact, the final words in the book of Nehemiah are "Remember me, O my God, for good" (Nehemiah 13:31). That's how I want to be remembered, too—in God's record and by God's people. For good.

In our moments of weakness, sometimes investing the energy required to strengthen our hands seems pointless. Sometimes we are tempted to question if it matters anyway.

It does matter. And finishing well is possible.

I think the New Testament leader whose leadership abilities most parallel Nehemiah's is the Apostle Paul. Paul served the Lord through almost every burden and obstacle imaginable.

…in labours more abundant, in stripes above measure, in prisons more frequent, in deaths oft. Of the Jews five times received I forty stripes save one. Thrice was I beaten with rods, once was I stoned, thrice I suffered shipwreck, a night and a day I have been in the deep; In journeyings often, in perils of waters, in perils of robbers, in perils by mine own countrymen, in perils by the heathen, in perils in the city, in perils in the wilderness, in perils in the sea, in perils among false brethren; In weariness and painfulness, in watchings often, in hunger and thirst, in fastings often, in cold and nakedness. Beside those things that are without, that which cometh upon me daily, the care of all the churches.
—2 Corinthians 11:23–28

But through it all, Paul was faithful. In Nehemiah's terms, he strengthened his hands. And because Paul's difficulties were ongoing and repetitive, he had to strengthen his hands again and again.

Was it worth it?

There is no way to even know the impact the Apostle Paul's ministry continues to have today. For starters, much of our New Testament was penned by Paul. Furthermore, most of the people I know are distant recipients of Paul's missionary journeys to the Gentiles.

But for Paul himself, as he prepared for the martyr's execution he expected, he could recount the past and look forward to the future with these words: "For I am now ready to be offered, and the time of my departure is at hand. I have fought a good fight, I have finished my course, I have kept the faith: Henceforth there is laid up for me a crown of righteousness, which the Lord, the righteous judge, shall give me at that day: and not to me only, but unto all them also that love his appearing" (2 Timothy 4:6–8).

I think he was glad he had strengthened his hands. And I think he still is.

Do you stand in a broken area of service with rubbish and ruins around you? Do you labor amidst the relentless opposition of critics? Do you face temptation to compromise your stand or your mission?

Strengthen your hands! The work is great, and the labor is heavy; but your God is able, and the reward is priceless.

One day, the wall will be finished. From the ramparts of Heaven, the trumpet will sound the ring of victory. Our Lord—who strengthened our hands—will appear. And we will be thankful we finished strong.

Until then, keep building.

PAUL CHAPPELL is the senior pastor of Lancaster Baptist Church and president of West Coast Baptist College in Lancaster, California. His biblical vision has led the church to become one of the most dynamic Baptist churches in the nation. His preaching is heard on Daily in the Word, a daily radio broadcast heard across America. Dr. Chappell has four children who are married and serving in Christian ministry. He has been married to his wife Terrie for over thirty years, and they have four married children and eight grandchildren. His children are all serving in Christian ministry.

You can connect with Dr. Chappell through his blog, Twitter, and Facebook:

paulchappell.com
twitter.com/paulchappell
facebook.com/pastor.paul.chappell

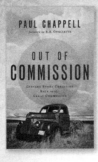
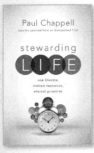

Visit us online

strivingtogether.com
wcbc.edu